this bucket list belongs to

_____

_____

"never give up because great things take time"

OUR BUCKET LIST

WE WANT TO DO THIS BECAUSE

_____
_____
_____
_____

OUR MEMORIES AND THOUGHTS

_____
_____
_____
_____
_____
_____
_____

COMPLETION DATE

_____

WOULD WE DO IT AGAIN?   YES ☐   NO ☐

OUR BUCKET LIST

WE WANT TO DO THIS BECAUSE

_____
_____
_____
_____

OUR MEMORIES AND THOUGHTS

_____
_____
_____
_____
_____
_____
_____
_____

COMPLETION DATE

_____

WOULD WE DO IT AGAIN?　　YES ☐　　NO ☐

OUR BUCKET LIST

WE WANT TO DO THIS BECAUSE

_____
_____
_____
_____

OUR MEMORIES AND THOUGHTS

_____
_____
_____
_____
_____
_____
_____
_____

COMPLETION DATE

_____

WOULD WE DO IT AGAIN?   YES ☐   NO ☐

OUR BUCKET LIST

WE WANT TO DO THIS BECAUSE

_____
_____
_____
_____

OUR MEMORIES AND THOUGHTS

_____
_____
_____
_____
_____
_____
_____
_____
_____

COMPLETION DATE

_____

WOULD WE DO IT AGAIN?   YES ☐   NO ☐

OUR BUCKET LIST

WE WANT TO DO THIS BECAUSE

_____
_____
_____
_____

OUR MEMORIES AND THOUGHTS

_____
_____
_____
_____
_____
_____
_____
_____

COMPLETION DATE

_____

WOULD WE DO IT AGAIN?   YES ☐   NO ☐

OUR BUCKET LIST

WE WANT TO DO THIS BECAUSE

_____
_____
_____
_____

OUR MEMORIES AND THOUGHTS

_____
_____
_____
_____
_____
_____
_____
_____

COMPLETION DATE

_____

WOULD WE DO IT AGAIN?   YES ☐   NO ☐

OUR BUCKET LIST

WE WANT TO DO THIS BECAUSE

_____
_____
_____
_____

OUR MEMORIES AND THOUGHTS

_____
_____
_____
_____
_____
_____
_____
_____

COMPLETION DATE

_____

WOULD WE DO IT AGAIN?   YES ☐   NO ☐

OUR BUCKET LIST

WE WANT TO DO THIS BECAUSE

_____
_____
_____
_____

OUR MEMORIES AND THOUGHTS

_____
_____
_____
_____
_____
_____
_____
_____

COMPLETION DATE

_____

WOULD WE DO IT AGAIN? YES ☐ NO ☐

OUR BUCKET LIST

WE WANT TO DO THIS BECAUSE

_____
_____
_____
_____

OUR MEMORIES AND THOUGHTS

_____
_____
_____
_____
_____
_____
_____
_____

COMPLETION DATE

_____

WOULD WE DO IT AGAIN?   YES ☐   NO ☐

OUR BUCKET LIST

WE WANT TO DO THIS BECAUSE

_____
_____
_____
_____

OUR MEMORIES AND THOUGHTS

_____
_____
_____
_____
_____
_____
_____
_____

COMPLETION DATE

_____

WOULD WE DO IT AGAIN?   YES ☐   NO ☐

OUR BUCKET LIST

WE WANT TO DO THIS BECAUSE

_____
_____
_____
_____

OUR MEMORIES AND THOUGHTS

_____
_____
_____
_____
_____
_____
_____
_____

COMPLETION DATE
_____

WOULD WE DO IT AGAIN?   YES ☐   NO ☐

OUR BUCKET LIST

WE WANT TO DO THIS BECAUSE

_____
_____
_____
_____
_____

OUR MEMORIES AND THOUGHTS

_____
_____
_____
_____
_____
_____
_____
_____
_____

COMPLETION DATE

_____

WOULD WE DO IT AGAIN?   YES ☐   NO ☐

OUR BUCKET LIST

WE WANT TO DO THIS BECAUSE

_____
_____
_____
_____

OUR MEMORIES AND THOUGHTS

_____
_____
_____
_____
_____
_____
_____
_____

COMPLETION DATE

_____

WOULD WE DO IT AGAIN?   YES ☐   NO ☐

OUR BUCKET LIST

WE WANT TO DO THIS BECAUSE

_____
_____
_____
_____

OUR MEMORIES AND THOUGHTS

_____
_____
_____
_____
_____
_____
_____
_____

COMPLETION DATE

_____

WOULD WE DO IT AGAIN?   YES ☐   NO ☐

OUR BUCKET LIST

WE WANT TO DO THIS BECAUSE

_____
_____
_____

OUR MEMORIES AND THOUGHTS

_____
_____
_____
_____
_____
_____
_____

COMPLETION DATE

_____

WOULD WE DO IT AGAIN?   YES ☐   NO ☐

OUR BUCKET LIST

WE WANT TO DO THIS BECAUSE

_____
_____
_____
_____

OUR MEMORIES AND THOUGHTS

_____
_____
_____
_____
_____
_____
_____
_____

COMPLETION DATE

_____

WOULD WE DO IT AGAIN?   YES ☐   NO ☐

OUR BUCKET LIST

WE WANT TO DO THIS BECAUSE

_____
_____
_____
_____

OUR MEMORIES AND THOUGHTS

_____
_____
_____
_____
_____
_____
_____
_____

COMPLETION DATE

_____

WOULD WE DO IT AGAIN?   YES ☐   NO ☐

OUR BUCKET LIST

WE WANT TO DO THIS BECAUSE

_____
_____
_____
_____

OUR MEMORIES AND THOUGHTS

_____
_____
_____
_____
_____
_____
_____
_____

COMPLETION DATE

_____

WOULD WE DO IT AGAIN?   YES ☐   NO ☐

OUR BUCKET LIST

WE WANT TO DO THIS BECAUSE

_____
_____
_____
_____

OUR MEMORIES AND THOUGHTS

_____
_____
_____
_____
_____
_____
_____
_____

COMPLETION DATE

_____

WOULD WE DO IT AGAIN?   YES ☐   NO ☐

OUR BUCKET LIST

WE WANT TO DO THIS BECAUSE

_____
_____
_____
_____

OUR MEMORIES AND THOUGHTS

_____
_____
_____
_____
_____
_____
_____
_____

COMPLETION DATE

_____

WOULD WE DO IT AGAIN?   YES ☐   NO ☐

OUR BUCKET LIST

WE WANT TO DO THIS BECAUSE

_____
_____
_____
_____

OUR MEMORIES AND THOUGHTS

_____
_____
_____
_____
_____
_____
_____
_____

COMPLETION DATE

_____

WOULD WE DO IT AGAIN?   YES ☐   NO ☐

OUR BUCKET LIST

WE WANT TO DO THIS BECAUSE

_____
_____
_____
_____

OUR MEMORIES AND THOUGHTS

_____
_____
_____
_____
_____
_____
_____

COMPLETION DATE

_____

WOULD WE DO IT AGAIN?   YES ☐   NO ☐

OUR BUCKET LIST

WE WANT TO DO THIS BECAUSE

_____
_____
_____
_____

OUR MEMORIES AND THOUGHTS

_____
_____
_____
_____
_____
_____
_____
_____

COMPLETION DATE

_____

WOULD WE DO IT AGAIN?   YES ☐   NO ☐

OUR BUCKET LIST

WE WANT TO DO THIS BECAUSE

_____
_____
_____
_____

OUR MEMORIES AND THOUGHTS

_____
_____
_____
_____
_____
_____
_____

COMPLETION DATE

_____

WOULD WE DO IT AGAIN?   YES ☐   NO ☐

OUR BUCKET LIST

WE WANT TO DO THIS BECAUSE

_____
_____
_____
_____
_____

OUR MEMORIES AND THOUGHTS

_____
_____
_____
_____
_____
_____
_____
_____

COMPLETION DATE

_____

WOULD WE DO IT AGAIN?   YES ☐   NO ☐

OUR BUCKET LIST

WE WANT TO DO THIS BECAUSE

_____
_____
_____
_____

OUR MEMORIES AND THOUGHTS

_____
_____
_____
_____
_____
_____
_____
_____

COMPLETION DATE

_____

WOULD WE DO IT AGAIN?   YES ☐   NO ☐

OUR BUCKET LIST

WE WANT TO DO THIS BECAUSE

_____
_____
_____
_____

OUR MEMORIES AND THOUGHTS

_____
_____
_____
_____
_____
_____
_____
_____

COMPLETION DATE

_____

WOULD WE DO IT AGAIN?   YES ☐   NO ☐

OUR BUCKET LIST

WE WANT TO DO THIS BECAUSE

_____
_____
_____
_____

OUR MEMORIES AND THOUGHTS

_____
_____
_____
_____
_____
_____
_____
_____

COMPLETION DATE

_____

WOULD WE DO IT AGAIN?   YES ☐   NO ☐

OUR BUCKET LIST

WE WANT TO DO THIS BECAUSE

_____
_____
_____
_____

OUR MEMORIES AND THOUGHTS

_____
_____
_____
_____
_____
_____
_____
_____

COMPLETION DATE

_____

WOULD WE DO IT AGAIN?   YES ☐   NO ☐

OUR BUCKET LIST

WE WANT TO DO THIS BECAUSE

_____
_____
_____
_____

OUR MEMORIES AND THOUGHTS

_____
_____
_____
_____
_____
_____
_____
_____

COMPLETION DATE

_____

WOULD WE DO IT AGAIN?   YES ☐   NO ☐

OUR BUCKET LIST

WE WANT TO DO THIS BECAUSE

_____
_____
_____
_____

OUR MEMORIES AND THOUGHTS

_____
_____
_____
_____
_____
_____
_____
_____

COMPLETION DATE

_____

WOULD WE DO IT AGAIN?   YES ☐   NO ☐

OUR BUCKET LIST

WE WANT TO DO THIS BECAUSE

_____
_____
_____
_____

OUR MEMORIES AND THOUGHTS

_____
_____
_____
_____
_____
_____
_____
_____

COMPLETION DATE

_____

WOULD WE DO IT AGAIN?　　YES ☐　　NO ☐

OUR BUCKET LIST

WE WANT TO DO THIS BECAUSE

_____
_____
_____
_____

OUR MEMORIES AND THOUGHTS

_____
_____
_____
_____
_____
_____
_____
_____

COMPLETION DATE

_____

WOULD WE DO IT AGAIN?   YES ☐   NO ☐

OUR BUCKET LIST

WE WANT TO DO THIS BECAUSE

_____
_____
_____
_____
_____

OUR MEMORIES AND THOUGHTS

_____
_____
_____
_____
_____
_____
_____
_____
_____

COMPLETION DATE

_____

WOULD WE DO IT AGAIN?　　YES ☐　　NO ☐

OUR BUCKET LIST

WE WANT TO DO THIS BECAUSE

_____
_____
_____
_____

OUR MEMORIES AND THOUGHTS

_____
_____
_____
_____
_____
_____
_____
_____

COMPLETION DATE

_____

WOULD WE DO IT AGAIN?   YES ☐   NO ☐

OUR BUCKET LIST

WE WANT TO DO THIS BECAUSE

_____
_____
_____
_____

OUR MEMORIES AND THOUGHTS

_____
_____
_____
_____
_____
_____
_____
_____

COMPLETION DATE

_____

WOULD WE DO IT AGAIN?   YES ☐   NO ☐

OUR BUCKET LIST

WE WANT TO DO THIS BECAUSE

_____
_____
_____
_____

OUR MEMORIES AND THOUGHTS

_____
_____
_____
_____
_____
_____
_____
_____

COMPLETION DATE

_____

WOULD WE DO IT AGAIN? YES ☐ NO ☐

OUR BUCKET LIST

WE WANT TO DO THIS BECAUSE

_____
_____
_____
_____

OUR MEMORIES AND THOUGHTS

_____
_____
_____
_____
_____
_____
_____
_____

COMPLETION DATE

_____

WOULD WE DO IT AGAIN?   YES ☐   NO ☐

OUR BUCKET LIST

WE WANT TO DO THIS BECAUSE

_____
_____
_____
_____

OUR MEMORIES AND THOUGHTS

_____
_____
_____
_____
_____
_____
_____
_____

COMPLETION DATE

_____

WOULD WE DO IT AGAIN?   YES ☐   NO ☐

OUR BUCKET LIST

WE WANT TO DO THIS BECAUSE

_____
_____
_____
_____

OUR MEMORIES AND THOUGHTS

_____
_____
_____
_____
_____
_____
_____
_____

COMPLETION DATE

_____

WOULD WE DO IT AGAIN?   YES ☐   NO ☐

OUR BUCKET LIST

WE WANT TO DO THIS BECAUSE

_____
_____
_____
_____

OUR MEMORIES AND THOUGHTS

_____
_____
_____
_____
_____
_____
_____
_____

COMPLETION DATE
_____

WOULD WE DO IT AGAIN?   YES ☐   NO ☐

OUR BUCKET LIST

WE WANT TO DO THIS BECAUSE

_____
_____
_____
_____

OUR MEMORIES AND THOUGHTS

_____
_____
_____
_____
_____
_____
_____
_____

COMPLETION DATE

_____

WOULD WE DO IT AGAIN?　　YES ☐　　NO ☐

OUR BUCKET LIST

WE WANT TO DO THIS BECAUSE

_____
_____
_____

OUR MEMORIES AND THOUGHTS

_____
_____
_____
_____
_____
_____
_____
_____

COMPLETION DATE

_____

WOULD WE DO IT AGAIN?   YES ☐   NO ☐

OUR BUCKET LIST

WE WANT TO DO THIS BECAUSE

_____
_____
_____
_____
_____

OUR MEMORIES AND THOUGHTS

_____
_____
_____
_____
_____
_____
_____
_____
_____

COMPLETION DATE

_____

WOULD WE DO IT AGAIN? YES ☐ NO ☐

OUR BUCKET LIST

WE WANT TO DO THIS BECAUSE

_____
_____
_____
_____

OUR MEMORIES AND THOUGHTS

_____
_____
_____
_____
_____
_____
_____
_____

COMPLETION DATE

_____

WOULD WE DO IT AGAIN?   YES ☐   NO ☐

OUR BUCKET LIST

WE WANT TO DO THIS BECAUSE

_____
_____
_____
_____

OUR MEMORIES AND THOUGHTS

_____
_____
_____
_____
_____
_____
_____
_____

COMPLETION DATE

_____

WOULD WE DO IT AGAIN?　　YES ☐　　NO ☐

OUR BUCKET LIST

WE WANT TO DO THIS BECAUSE

_____
_____
_____
_____

OUR MEMORIES AND THOUGHTS

_____
_____
_____
_____
_____
_____
_____
_____

COMPLETION DATE

_____

WOULD WE DO IT AGAIN?　　YES ☐　　NO ☐

OUR BUCKET LIST

WE WANT TO DO THIS BECAUSE

_____
_____
_____
_____
_____

OUR MEMORIES AND THOUGHTS

_____
_____
_____
_____
_____
_____
_____
_____
_____

COMPLETION DATE

_____

WOULD WE DO IT AGAIN?   YES ☐   NO ☐

OUR BUCKET LIST

WE WANT TO DO THIS BECAUSE

_____
_____
_____
_____

OUR MEMORIES AND THOUGHTS

_____
_____
_____
_____
_____
_____
_____
_____

COMPLETION DATE

_____

WOULD WE DO IT AGAIN?   YES ☐   NO ☐

OUR BUCKET LIST

WE WANT TO DO THIS BECAUSE

_____
_____
_____
_____

OUR MEMORIES AND THOUGHTS

_____
_____
_____
_____
_____
_____
_____

COMPLETION DATE

_____

WOULD WE DO IT AGAIN?   YES ☐   NO ☐

OUR BUCKET LIST

WE WANT TO DO THIS BECAUSE

_____
_____
_____
_____

OUR MEMORIES AND THOUGHTS

_____
_____
_____
_____
_____
_____
_____
_____

COMPLETION DATE

_____

WOULD WE DO IT AGAIN?   YES ☐   NO ☐

OUR BUCKET LIST

WE WANT TO DO THIS BECAUSE

_____
_____
_____
_____

OUR MEMORIES AND THOUGHTS

_____
_____
_____
_____
_____
_____
_____
_____
_____

COMPLETION DATE

_____

WOULD WE DO IT AGAIN?   YES ☐   NO ☐

OUR BUCKET LIST

WE WANT TO DO THIS BECAUSE

_____
_____
_____
_____

OUR MEMORIES AND THOUGHTS

_____
_____
_____
_____
_____
_____
_____
_____

COMPLETION DATE

_____

WOULD WE DO IT AGAIN?   YES ☐   NO ☐

OUR BUCKET LIST

WE WANT TO DO THIS BECAUSE

_____
_____
_____
_____

OUR MEMORIES AND THOUGHTS

_____
_____
_____
_____
_____
_____
_____
_____

COMPLETION DATE

_____

WOULD WE DO IT AGAIN?   YES ☐   NO ☐

OUR BUCKET LIST

WE WANT TO DO THIS BECAUSE

_____
_____
_____
_____

OUR MEMORIES AND THOUGHTS

_____
_____
_____
_____
_____
_____
_____
_____

COMPLETION DATE

_____

WOULD WE DO IT AGAIN?   YES ☐   NO ☐

OUR BUCKET LIST

WE WANT TO DO THIS BECAUSE

_____
_____
_____
_____
_____

OUR MEMORIES AND THOUGHTS

_____
_____
_____
_____
_____
_____
_____
_____

COMPLETION DATE

_____

WOULD WE DO IT AGAIN?   YES ☐   NO ☐

OUR BUCKET LIST

WE WANT TO DO THIS BECAUSE

_____
_____
_____
_____

OUR MEMORIES AND THOUGHTS

_____
_____
_____
_____
_____
_____
_____
_____

COMPLETION DATE

_____

WOULD WE DO IT AGAIN?   YES ☐   NO ☐

OUR BUCKET LIST

WE WANT TO DO THIS BECAUSE

_____
_____
_____
_____

OUR MEMORIES AND THOUGHTS

_____
_____
_____
_____
_____
_____
_____
_____

COMPLETION DATE

_____

WOULD WE DO IT AGAIN?   YES ☐   NO ☐

OUR BUCKET LIST

WE WANT TO DO THIS BECAUSE

_____
_____
_____
_____
_____

OUR MEMORIES AND THOUGHTS

_____
_____
_____
_____
_____
_____
_____
_____
_____

COMPLETION DATE

_____

WOULD WE DO IT AGAIN?   YES ☐   NO ☐

OUR BUCKET LIST

WE WANT TO DO THIS BECAUSE

_____
_____
_____
_____

OUR MEMORIES AND THOUGHTS

_____
_____
_____
_____
_____
_____
_____
_____

COMPLETION DATE

_____

WOULD WE DO IT AGAIN?   YES ☐   NO ☐

OUR BUCKET LIST

WE WANT TO DO THIS BECAUSE

OUR MEMORIES AND THOUGHTS

COMPLETION DATE

WOULD WE DO IT AGAIN? YES ☐   NO ☐

OUR BUCKET LIST

WE WANT TO DO THIS BECAUSE

_____
_____
_____
_____

OUR MEMORIES AND THOUGHTS

_____
_____
_____
_____
_____
_____
_____
_____

COMPLETION DATE

_____

WOULD WE DO IT AGAIN?　　YES ☐　　NO ☐

OUR BUCKET LIST

WE WANT TO DO THIS BECAUSE

_____
_____
_____
_____

OUR MEMORIES AND THOUGHTS

_____
_____
_____
_____
_____
_____
_____

COMPLETION DATE

_____

WOULD WE DO IT AGAIN?   YES ☐   NO ☐

OUR BUCKET LIST

WE WANT TO DO THIS BECAUSE

_____
_____
_____
_____

OUR MEMORIES AND THOUGHTS

_____
_____
_____
_____
_____
_____
_____
_____

COMPLETION DATE

_____

WOULD WE DO IT AGAIN?   YES ☐   NO ☐

OUR BUCKET LIST

WE WANT TO DO THIS BECAUSE

_____
_____
_____
_____

OUR MEMORIES AND THOUGHTS

_____
_____
_____
_____
_____
_____
_____
_____

COMPLETION DATE

_____

WOULD WE DO IT AGAIN?   YES ☐   NO ☐

OUR BUCKET LIST

WE WANT TO DO THIS BECAUSE

_____
_____
_____
_____

OUR MEMORIES AND THOUGHTS

_____
_____
_____
_____
_____
_____
_____
_____

COMPLETION DATE

_____

WOULD WE DO IT AGAIN?   YES ☐   NO ☐

OUR BUCKET LIST

WE WANT TO DO THIS BECAUSE

_____
_____
_____
_____

OUR MEMORIES AND THOUGHTS

_____
_____
_____
_____
_____
_____
_____
_____

COMPLETION DATE

_____

WOULD WE DO IT AGAIN?   YES ☐   NO ☐

OUR BUCKET LIST

WE WANT TO DO THIS BECAUSE

_____
_____
_____
_____

OUR MEMORIES AND THOUGHTS

_____
_____
_____
_____
_____
_____
_____
_____

COMPLETION DATE

_____

WOULD WE DO IT AGAIN? YES ☐ NO ☐

OUR BUCKET LIST

WE WANT TO DO THIS BECAUSE

_____
_____
_____
_____

OUR MEMORIES AND THOUGHTS

_____
_____
_____
_____
_____
_____
_____

COMPLETION DATE

_____

WOULD WE DO IT AGAIN?   YES ☐   NO ☐

OUR BUCKET LIST

WE WANT TO DO THIS BECAUSE

_____
_____
_____
_____

OUR MEMORIES AND THOUGHTS

_____
_____
_____
_____
_____
_____
_____
_____

COMPLETION DATE

_____

WOULD WE DO IT AGAIN?   YES ☐   NO ☐

OUR BUCKET LIST

WE WANT TO DO THIS BECAUSE

_____
_____
_____
_____

OUR MEMORIES AND THOUGHTS

_____
_____
_____
_____
_____
_____
_____
_____

COMPLETION DATE

_____

WOULD WE DO IT AGAIN?   YES ☐   NO ☐

OUR BUCKET LIST

WE WANT TO DO THIS BECAUSE

_____
_____
_____
_____

OUR MEMORIES AND THOUGHTS

_____
_____
_____
_____
_____
_____
_____
_____

COMPLETION DATE

_____

WOULD WE DO IT AGAIN?   YES ☐   NO ☐

OUR BUCKET LIST

WE WANT TO DO THIS BECAUSE

_____
_____
_____

OUR MEMORIES AND THOUGHTS

_____
_____
_____
_____
_____
_____
_____
_____

COMPLETION DATE

_____

WOULD WE DO IT AGAIN?   YES ☐   NO ☐

OUR BUCKET LIST

WE WANT TO DO THIS BECAUSE

_____
_____
_____
_____

OUR MEMORIES AND THOUGHTS

_____
_____
_____
_____
_____
_____
_____
_____

COMPLETION DATE

_____

WOULD WE DO IT AGAIN?   YES ☐   NO ☐

OUR BUCKET LIST

WE WANT TO DO THIS BECAUSE

_____
_____
_____
_____

OUR MEMORIES AND THOUGHTS

_____
_____
_____
_____
_____
_____
_____
_____

COMPLETION DATE

_____

WOULD WE DO IT AGAIN?   YES ☐   NO ☐

OUR BUCKET LIST

WE WANT TO DO THIS BECAUSE

_____
_____
_____
_____

OUR MEMORIES AND THOUGHTS

_____
_____
_____
_____
_____
_____
_____
_____

COMPLETION DATE

_____

WOULD WE DO IT AGAIN?   YES ☐   NO ☐

OUR BUCKET LIST

WE WANT TO DO THIS BECAUSE

_____

_____

_____

_____

OUR MEMORIES AND THOUGHTS

_____

_____

_____

_____

_____

_____

_____

_____

COMPLETION DATE

_____

WOULD WE DO IT AGAIN?   YES ☐   NO ☐

OUR BUCKET LIST

WE WANT TO DO THIS BECAUSE

_____
_____
_____
_____
_____

OUR MEMORIES AND THOUGHTS

_____
_____
_____
_____
_____
_____
_____
_____
_____
_____

COMPLETION DATE

_____

WOULD WE DO IT AGAIN?   YES ☐   NO ☐

OUR BUCKET LIST

WE WANT TO DO THIS BECAUSE

_____
_____
_____
_____

OUR MEMORIES AND THOUGHTS

_____
_____
_____
_____
_____
_____
_____
_____

COMPLETION DATE

_____

WOULD WE DO IT AGAIN?   YES ☐   NO ☐

OUR BUCKET LIST

WE WANT TO DO THIS BECAUSE

_____
_____
_____
_____

OUR MEMORIES AND THOUGHTS

_____
_____
_____
_____
_____
_____
_____
_____
_____

COMPLETION DATE

_____

WOULD WE DO IT AGAIN?   YES ☐   NO ☐

OUR BUCKET LIST

WE WANT TO DO THIS BECAUSE

_____
_____
_____
_____

OUR MEMORIES AND THOUGHTS

_____
_____
_____
_____
_____
_____
_____
_____

COMPLETION DATE

_____

WOULD WE DO IT AGAIN?   YES ☐   NO ☐

OUR BUCKET LIST

WE WANT TO DO THIS BECAUSE

_____
_____
_____
_____

OUR MEMORIES AND THOUGHTS

_____
_____
_____
_____
_____
_____
_____
_____
_____

COMPLETION DATE

_____

WOULD WE DO IT AGAIN?   YES ☐   NO ☐

OUR BUCKET LIST

WE WANT TO DO THIS BECAUSE

_____
_____
_____
_____

OUR MEMORIES AND THOUGHTS

_____
_____
_____
_____
_____
_____
_____
_____

COMPLETION DATE

_____

WOULD WE DO IT AGAIN?   YES ☐   NO ☐

OUR BUCKET LIST

WE WANT TO DO THIS BECAUSE

_____
_____
_____
_____

OUR MEMORIES AND THOUGHTS

_____
_____
_____
_____
_____
_____
_____
_____

COMPLETION DATE

_____

WOULD WE DO IT AGAIN?　　YES ☐　　NO ☐

OUR BUCKET LIST

WE WANT TO DO THIS BECAUSE

_____
_____
_____
_____
_____

OUR MEMORIES AND THOUGHTS

_____
_____
_____
_____
_____
_____
_____
_____
_____
_____

COMPLETION DATE

_____

WOULD WE DO IT AGAIN?　　YES ☐　　NO ☐

OUR BUCKET LIST

WE WANT TO DO THIS BECAUSE

_____
_____
_____
_____

OUR MEMORIES AND THOUGHTS

_____
_____
_____
_____
_____
_____
_____
_____

COMPLETION DATE

_____

WOULD WE DO IT AGAIN?   YES ☐   NO ☐

OUR BUCKET LIST

WE WANT TO DO THIS BECAUSE

_____
_____
_____
_____

OUR MEMORIES AND THOUGHTS

_____
_____
_____
_____
_____
_____
_____
_____

COMPLETION DATE

_____

WOULD WE DO IT AGAIN?   YES ☐   NO ☐

OUR BUCKET LIST

WE WANT TO DO THIS BECAUSE

_____
_____
_____
_____

OUR MEMORIES AND THOUGHTS

_____
_____
_____
_____
_____
_____
_____
_____

COMPLETION DATE

_____

WOULD WE DO IT AGAIN?   YES ☐   NO ☐

OUR BUCKET LIST

WE WANT TO DO THIS BECAUSE

_____
_____
_____
_____

OUR MEMORIES AND THOUGHTS

_____
_____
_____
_____
_____
_____
_____
_____

COMPLETION DATE

_____

WOULD WE DO IT AGAIN?   YES ☐   NO ☐

OUR BUCKET LIST

WE WANT TO DO THIS BECAUSE

_____
_____
_____
_____

OUR MEMORIES AND THOUGHTS

_____
_____
_____
_____
_____
_____
_____
_____

COMPLETION DATE

_____

WOULD WE DO IT AGAIN?   YES ☐   NO ☐

OUR BUCKET LIST

WE WANT TO DO THIS BECAUSE

_____
_____
_____
_____

OUR MEMORIES AND THOUGHTS

_____
_____
_____
_____
_____
_____
_____
_____

COMPLETION DATE

_____

WOULD WE DO IT AGAIN?　　YES ☐　　NO ☐

OUR BUCKET LIST

WE WANT TO DO THIS BECAUSE

_____
_____
_____
_____

OUR MEMORIES AND THOUGHTS

_____
_____
_____
_____
_____
_____
_____
_____

COMPLETION DATE

_____

WOULD WE DO IT AGAIN?   YES ☐   NO ☐

OUR BUCKET LIST

WE WANT TO DO THIS BECAUSE

_____
_____
_____
_____

OUR MEMORIES AND THOUGHTS

_____
_____
_____
_____
_____
_____
_____
_____

COMPLETION DATE

_____

WOULD WE DO IT AGAIN?   YES ☐   NO ☐

OUR BUCKET LIST

WE WANT TO DO THIS BECAUSE

_____
_____
_____
_____

OUR MEMORIES AND THOUGHTS

_____
_____
_____
_____
_____
_____
_____
_____

COMPLETION DATE

_____

WOULD WE DO IT AGAIN?   YES ☐   NO ☐

OUR BUCKET LIST

WE WANT TO DO THIS BECAUSE

_____
_____
_____
_____

OUR MEMORIES AND THOUGHTS

_____
_____
_____
_____
_____
_____
_____
_____

COMPLETION DATE

_____

WOULD WE DO IT AGAIN? YES ☐   NO ☐

OUR BUCKET LIST

WE WANT TO DO THIS BECAUSE

_____
_____
_____
_____

OUR MEMORIES AND THOUGHTS

_____
_____
_____
_____
_____
_____
_____
_____

COMPLETION DATE

_____

WOULD WE DO IT AGAIN?   YES ☐   NO ☐

OUR BUCKET LIST

WE WANT TO DO THIS BECAUSE

_____
_____
_____
_____

OUR MEMORIES AND THOUGHTS

_____
_____
_____
_____
_____
_____
_____
_____

COMPLETION DATE

_____

WOULD WE DO IT AGAIN?   YES ☐   NO ☐

OUR BUCKET LIST

WE WANT TO DO THIS BECAUSE

_____
_____
_____
_____
_____

OUR MEMORIES AND THOUGHTS

_____
_____
_____
_____
_____
_____
_____
_____
_____

COMPLETION DATE

_____

WOULD WE DO IT AGAIN?   YES ☐   NO ☐

OUR BUCKET LIST

WE WANT TO DO THIS BECAUSE

_____
_____
_____
_____

OUR MEMORIES AND THOUGHTS

_____
_____
_____
_____
_____
_____
_____

COMPLETION DATE

_____

WOULD WE DO IT AGAIN?   YES ☐   NO ☐

OUR BUCKET LIST

WE WANT TO DO THIS BECAUSE

_____
_____
_____
_____

OUR MEMORIES AND THOUGHTS

_____
_____
_____
_____
_____
_____
_____
_____

COMPLETION DATE

_____

WOULD WE DO IT AGAIN?   YES ☐   NO ☐

OUR BUCKET LIST

WE WANT TO DO THIS BECAUSE

_____
_____
_____
_____

OUR MEMORIES AND THOUGHTS

_____
_____
_____
_____
_____
_____
_____
_____

COMPLETION DATE

_____

WOULD WE DO IT AGAIN?   YES ☐   NO ☐

OUR BUCKET LIST

WE WANT TO DO THIS BECAUSE

_____
_____
_____
_____

OUR MEMORIES AND THOUGHTS

_____
_____
_____
_____
_____
_____
_____
_____

COMPLETION DATE

_____

WOULD WE DO IT AGAIN?   YES ☐   NO ☐

OUR BUCKET LIST

WE WANT TO DO THIS BECAUSE

_____
_____
_____
_____

OUR MEMORIES AND THOUGHTS

_____
_____
_____
_____
_____
_____
_____
_____

COMPLETION DATE

_____

WOULD WE DO IT AGAIN?   YES ☐   NO ☐

OUR BUCKET LIST

WE WANT TO DO THIS BECAUSE

_____
_____
_____
_____
_____

OUR MEMORIES AND THOUGHTS

_____
_____
_____
_____
_____
_____
_____
_____
_____

COMPLETION DATE

_____

WOULD WE DO IT AGAIN?　　YES ☐　　NO ☐

OUR BUCKET LIST

WE WANT TO DO THIS BECAUSE

_____
_____
_____
_____

OUR MEMORIES AND THOUGHTS

_____
_____
_____
_____
_____
_____
_____
_____

COMPLETION DATE

_____

WOULD WE DO IT AGAIN?   YES ☐   NO ☐

OUR BUCKET LIST

WE WANT TO DO THIS BECAUSE

_____
_____
_____
_____

OUR MEMORIES AND THOUGHTS

_____
_____
_____
_____
_____
_____
_____
_____

COMPLETION DATE

_____

WOULD WE DO IT AGAIN?   YES ☐   NO ☐

OUR BUCKET LIST

WE WANT TO DO THIS BECAUSE

_____
_____
_____
_____

OUR MEMORIES AND THOUGHTS

_____
_____
_____
_____
_____
_____
_____
_____

COMPLETION DATE

_____

WOULD WE DO IT AGAIN?   YES ☐   NO ☐

OUR BUCKET LIST

WE WANT TO DO THIS BECAUSE

_____
_____
_____
_____

OUR MEMORIES AND THOUGHTS

_____
_____
_____
_____
_____
_____
_____
_____

COMPLETION DATE

_____

WOULD WE DO IT AGAIN?   YES ☐   NO ☐

OUR BUCKET LIST

WE WANT TO DO THIS BECAUSE

_____
_____
_____
_____

OUR MEMORIES AND THOUGHTS

_____
_____
_____
_____
_____
_____
_____
_____

COMPLETION DATE

_____

WOULD WE DO IT AGAIN?   YES ☐   NO ☐

OUR BUCKET LIST

WE WANT TO DO THIS BECAUSE

_____
_____
_____
_____

OUR MEMORIES AND THOUGHTS

_____
_____
_____
_____
_____
_____
_____
_____

COMPLETION DATE

_____

WOULD WE DO IT AGAIN?   YES ☐   NO ☐

OUR BUCKET LIST

WE WANT TO DO THIS BECAUSE

_____
_____
_____
_____

OUR MEMORIES AND THOUGHTS

_____
_____
_____
_____
_____
_____
_____
_____

COMPLETION DATE

_____

WOULD WE DO IT AGAIN? YES ☐ NO ☐

OUR BUCKET LIST

WE WANT TO DO THIS BECAUSE

_____
_____
_____
_____

OUR MEMORIES AND THOUGHTS

_____
_____
_____
_____
_____
_____
_____
_____

COMPLETION DATE

_____

WOULD WE DO IT AGAIN?   YES ☐   NO ☐

OUR BUCKET LIST

WE WANT TO DO THIS BECAUSE

_____
_____
_____
_____

OUR MEMORIES AND THOUGHTS

_____
_____
_____
_____
_____
_____
_____
_____

COMPLETION DATE

_____

WOULD WE DO IT AGAIN?   YES ☐   NO ☐

OUR BUCKET LIST

WE WANT TO DO THIS BECAUSE

_____
_____
_____
_____

OUR MEMORIES AND THOUGHTS

_____
_____
_____
_____
_____
_____
_____
_____

COMPLETION DATE

_____

WOULD WE DO IT AGAIN? YES ☐   NO ☐

OUR BUCKET LIST

WE WANT TO DO THIS BECAUSE

OUR MEMORIES AND THOUGHTS

COMPLETION DATE

WOULD WE DO IT AGAIN?   YES ☐   NO ☐

OUR BUCKET LIST

WE WANT TO DO THIS BECAUSE

_____
_____
_____
_____

OUR MEMORIES AND THOUGHTS

_____
_____
_____
_____
_____
_____
_____
_____

COMPLETION DATE

_____

WOULD WE DO IT AGAIN?   YES ☐   NO ☐

OUR BUCKET LIST

WE WANT TO DO THIS BECAUSE

_____
_____
_____
_____

OUR MEMORIES AND THOUGHTS

_____
_____
_____
_____
_____
_____
_____

COMPLETION DATE

_____

WOULD WE DO IT AGAIN?   YES ☐   NO ☐

OUR BUCKET LIST

WE WANT TO DO THIS BECAUSE

_____
_____
_____
_____

OUR MEMORIES AND THOUGHTS

_____
_____
_____
_____
_____
_____
_____
_____

COMPLETION DATE

_____

WOULD WE DO IT AGAIN?   YES ☐   NO ☐

OUR BUCKET LIST

WE WANT TO DO THIS BECAUSE

_____
_____
_____
_____
_____

OUR MEMORIES AND THOUGHTS

_____
_____
_____
_____
_____
_____
_____
_____
_____

COMPLETION DATE

_____

WOULD WE DO IT AGAIN?　　YES ☐　　NO ☐

CPSIA information can be obtained
at www.ICGtesting.com
Printed in the USA
LVHW080048130221
679116LV00002BA/530